Wayfare

Wayfare

Pattiann Rogers

PENGUIN POETS

PENGUIN BOOKS

Published by the Penguin Group

Penguin Group (USA) Inc., 375 Hudson Street, New York, New York 10014, U.S.A.
Penguin Group (Canada), 90 Eglinton Avenue East, Suite 700, Toronto, Ontario, Canada M4P 2Y3
(a division of Pearson Penguin Canada Inc.)
Penguin Books Ltd, 80 Strand, London WC2R 0RL, England
Penguin Ireland, 25 St Stephen's Green, Dublin 2, Ireland (a division of Penguin Books Ltd)
Penguin Group (Australia), 250 Camberwell Road, Camberwell, Victoria 3124, Australia
(a division of Pearson Australia Group Pty Ltd)
Penguin Books India Pvt Ltd, 11 Community Centre, Panchsheel Park, New Delhi – 110 017, India
Penguin Group (NZ), 67 Apollo Drive, Rosedale, North Shore 0632, New Zealand
(a division of Pearson New Zealand Ltd)
Penguin Books (South Africa) (Pty) Ltd, 24 Sturdee Avenue, Rosebank, Johannesburg 2196,
South Africa

Penguin Books Ltd, Registered Offices:
80 Strand, London WC2R 0RL, England

First published in Penguin Books 2008

10 9 8 7 6 5 4 3 2 1

Page 113 constitutes an extension of this copyright page.

ISBN 978-0-14-311334-8
CIP data available

Printed in the United States of America
Set in New Caledonia
Designed by Ginger Legato

For my husband,

and in memory of my uncle, "Unk,"
Floyd G. Keiter, 1920–2006

Contents

Symposium Center

Sanctuary

Theater

Natural History Exposition

Wayfare

The Great Deluge and Its Coming

We were tangled together and carried
roughly by the vicious
waters, thrown about, buffeted cruelly

in the racing surge. We were a snarl of bald pates, bellies
and spines with their multiple links,
all wound together,
a bolus, hairy bodies, snouts of fur, woolly
appendages, scaly appendages, fingers,
hooves, claws, a clamor of sputterings,
groans, and screeches
tumbling over and over, each of us surfacing

momentarily, taking air from the sky,
then submerged again, tossed, undone, entwined anew.

Two spider monkeys, dripping and wheezing,
scrambled
over my head for a place on top.
A hoary marmot
grabbed my ankle, slipped, caught a scrabble
of branches drifting by carrying a rooster and corn snake.

A weasel-like
creature curled around my neck, jumped
to the grizzled back of a warthog thrashing
in the wake. What was it
clawing and clutching at my shoulder?

Once, in the flooding mayhem, I came face-to-face
with a blue-faced mandrill
and his fear-whitened eyes. Once a spotted bat grasped
my collar, hung there until I was hit by a wave

and wrenched away clinging upside
                    down to a mule braying its harsh treble.

    For a distance a dog, a dingo, held on
                                        by her teeth clamped to the belt
            at my waist. I circled her mangy head
                    with one arm, clung with the other
                                        to the bulk of a musk ox
        pitching past
                    in the swell. Seeds and nuts and the roots
            of tundra grasses were matted in his long
                            hanging fur, among which roots crouched
            numerous mice harboring nits and fleas
                                    and wingless flies.

                    We were mewing
        and choking, spitting
                            and barking in our plight, the bundle
    of us in a jumble, struggling, shifting constantly, losing hold
                                    in white water, breaking apart,

                            carried away, found again. We were
        knocked and shaken, buffeted against rocks,
                                    engulfed flailing,
            swung into shore by the current and jerked out
                    to mid-torrent again by the same.
                    Direction was destiny.

    But were those really white wings spread wide,
                gliding silently over us
                            all the way in the tumult?
            Or was it simply a deeper heaven of moonlit clouds calm
                    in a certain prophecy
            that hovered above us through the night?

Or was it the ultimate stillness of the dependable void
                                         that kept us comforted
       until we were brought, finally floating
                              slowly together, almost sleeping,
                 into a growing light burning and blinding
like the conflagration of dawn over an open sea?

Concert Hall

Recitative from *The Ruby Plan*, Act I, Scene iv

I had a room once. The half-paneled
walls were of brown wood, waxed
until just on the edge of going
to gold, just on the verge of retreating
to black. The corner windows
I kept shuttered with a similar wood.
And above the panels, the walls
were a paisley-patterned madras
of bleeding red, wine, purple.

My single lamp, of deep red
cut glass studded and baubled,
sat on the bureau holding fire.

I myself was made of rose glass
blown and shaped. I wore long
strings of glass magenta beads
that glinted and clinked against
my body when I moved. The light
shone through me always thrice
with a red hue, blue-red at those
throbbing points most attractive.
I cast no shadow.

I was always happy whenever one
of them entered my room, reflecting
red off his body, in his eyes, the clever
way each had of removing my several
beaded necklaces, hanging them
on the bedpost or draping them in scallops
across the shutters. One of the wittiest
wound the sharp glittering strings
around his waist and mine until we
were pulled close and bound together.

My clear happiness was transparent
in those times, but I saved my most
thoroughly hidden ardor for the boy
who came with the emerald-deep
caresses of the sea, whose fragrances
were of the sapphire sky, whose face
held and reflected above me so that I
could see for myself the multifaceted
lightning and stone shadows of my soul,
the boy whose pearl-smooth belly
I knew to love best with my ruby lips.

The Metal Lion and the Monk, a Percussion Quintet
(cymbals, marimba, Earth gong, snare drum, and triangle, with tenor voice)

When he lifts his head from sleep
and stretches to rise, there's an enormity
of creaking in the landscape, gear against
gear, axle and cross, a slow grating
vibration shuddering the inner hills,
lisping and whining the dull pines,
cranking the tidal seas. I have learned
to recognize it.

His paws, moving with deliberation
against rock, create sparks
by which he marks his own way
among boulders at night. I have seen him
set dry kindling and parched brush
to flame by the pace of his journey.
The grace he covets is in the easy
glide of the iron gray flanks
he sometimes sees bounding with thunder
across the wet heavens.

His verses ring like underwater
triangles of steel struck with slender
rods, like the shadows of brass gongs
shaken in distant mountain caves.

His soul is the tensile measure
of his skeleton and skull, no more
material than the glistening,
like aluminum moonlight, of his smooth
mane and molded body in rain.

If he is merciful, it is with a mercy
as welded and steady as girders
and beams. If he is righteous,
it is with a righteousness burning like plates
of copper sun flaring off swift rivers.

I myself become rich when he gazes
into my devotions with his silver eyes,
when he soothes with his gold tongue
every crevice of my incantations.
He loves with all the potential forms
that metal can assume.

Even in his own realm, he has a place
in the corridors of this monastery.
I remember him in his virtues and plights.
I pray to his god to take notice.

Symphony in Three Movements

I. Lost in the Heart of the Concert

I thread through the assembly,
between the rows of violins,
the ritual bows rising and falling.
I confess to the oboes, counsel
with the wisdom of the flutes,
linger in the church of the momentarily
stilled tambourines and timpani.

All the while Satan in white
satin tux follows me silently,
his white patent leather pumps
with the soft soles keeping time
almost imperceptibly to the beat
of the baton at the altar.
His synchronization is perfect.

I try to avoid him, wandering
the hallways between the intoning
of the cellos, hiding among
the statuesque faith of the bass
fiddles. I draw the nearest one
to me, feel its deep strum
in my belly, press against its length
as if to disappear into its body.
He peers straight at me
through the strings of the harp.

He understands, he forgives.
Abiding and patient, he spies
on me in the blue of his pale
eyes as I kneel praying
with the woodwinds. He seems

to pray himself; beseeching
it appears. He stays so close
I can smell the ice-cold silver
of his hair, his boutonniere
of violets, an occasional
scent of rare whiskey.

He willingly enters the cadence
of heaven beside me. I allow him.
He hums by heart, along
with my heart, the good news
of the horns, the hallowed
score of the first and second violas.
He is becoming the clean white
seed of reverence. He takes
my hand. Neither I nor the flaring
sun of the trumpets can detect
any longer his black glass skeleton.
He kisses my cheek. I say he is
as innocent and constant as beauty.

No canticle, no hymn of salvation
from the celestial, can ever save us now.

II. The Flavor of the Composition

The arrangement opens
in adagio with sliced apples,
fennel and chicory. Ham
and comté enter with fanfare
immediately against a background
score of modulated grapeseed oil,
brushed cymbal of cider vinegar,
and the harmony of honey
punctuated by the occasional
beat of mustard and staccato
of poppy seeds. The finale
is highlighted by the sturdy
bass pizzicato of pecans, three
trills of parsley, the entire ensemble
moving, with strategically placed
rests and pauses, through theme
and time until the last chord.

III. By These Concerted Means: The Bellringer's Gift

Unlocking the three locks,
each as large as his hand, he opens
the heavy doors to the tower,
steps into the secrecy room, the cross
rib vaulting high above him,
the chest of treasured documents
chained to the floor in the corner.

He begins to climb the first
flight of wooden stairs, passing
the copper-plated dragon leaning
over the landing guarding the way,
the threat of its huge gaping jaws,
up to the second floor where
four stone soldiers stand on watch
facing in four directions, and up
the next flight, the creak and dust,
up to the housing of the clock, its multiple
weights suspended by their cords
from the height of the rafters, and on up
to the top, up to the chamber where
the great bell hangs silent and cold.

Then out into the sky by the forged
metal and its consecration, by the tower
and the open windows of the belfry,
by the rope he takes in his hands and pulls
and releases and pulls and releases,
so travels the peal of this voice
he is given and the gift of its language,
a herald proclaiming in a foreign tongue
from a strange and distant world.

Overture to the Operetta *Love at Sea*

Here, in brief, are the themes to come:
one moving like a permanent green
swale of meadow sea between bird-
covered cliffs; one moving like the blue,
stained-glass shimmer of reef fish
swimming through sun like sun passing
through stained glass as blue-violet
fish of light swimming on the wall;
another theme gliding in repetition
like a line of floating primrose petals,
tone by tone; another moving
with the equanimity of a sine curve,
the curved hip of a cumulus cloud
in reflection, two thighs defined
in the fat roll and parting of a wave.

Scripture is not pronounced
in this province but performed. Thus eye
of the blind, foot of the lame, crippled
tongue, these matter little in the swell
and list of this affair. Listen to the motif.
Some call it healing, some transfiguration,
some conception over deep water.

As black and white are simply two
sides of the same moon, so in this realm
the hand and the caress are a single
virtue. Like a mermaid's fan closing
and opening before her face as she turns
to dive, life and death exist here in union.
You might at any time go to sleep in one
and wake, as underwater, wholly in the other.

Move into the argument of these refrains
as if down into the sea, a parting
of primrose thighs, as if a swale of sun
down into love. Such are the places
expostulated by the motion of sound
performed in these measures to come.

The Lost Virtuoso and His Violin

Its case is perfect—pre-formed
laminated wood shell, padded red
velvet lining, matching satin-backed
blanket fringed. The pillowed interior
is molded to fit exactly the scroll,
tuning pegs, sounding board, formed
perfectly to accommodate its shape
and function, had it ever been.

He stands in the room, before
the window, before the mirror, before
this testament, head tilted, arm lifted
prepared to cradle the slender weight,
empty hand curved lightly for the bow.
He would be its countenance. It would be
his attention. He knows the technique.

He recalls his recollection of the vista
they might create together on the corner
in April, the streetlamp just brightening
at dusk, how their music would draw all
who passed, how the people would gladly
place flowers and coins on the velvet
of the open case for the memories of the music,
had the music ever been known.

He believes in the possible fire inside
its body. He almost remembers how
it would have kept him warm in winter
with the hum of its heat held beneath
his chin, against his chest. They could
have consorted, reminisced together,
each listening to the other in the deaf
and diligent snow, had there been fire,

had he ever held it close. He could have
given it declaration. It could have delivered
him far beyond the icy solstice.

He unlatches the case often at night,
laying it open. He closes his eyes,
touches the red satin, the velvet, his fingers
moving, almost like a music, tracing
the shape of the emptiness formed
to fit his heaven, its absence his mission,
his mission his madness.

The Sun in the Home for Retired Musicians

The stained-glass window in the parlor
off the entrance attracts them all. Each resident
feels a freedom of memory gazing at that abstract
mosaic of colors. The arrangement of translucent
scarlet and purple chips, slivers, beads of blue
sea and evening sun-corals recalls for each
a certain sequence of notes, a perfect pitch,
an elevation of performance.

Like gazing at a pattern of sounds, each hears again
the shimmering suns of the brass, the shifting
greens and darker forests of the strings, the strike
and the pause coming together to create a suggestion
of conjunction in a time of fixed space.

Sitting in that place, an aging maestro nods, humming
a line of lavender against gold. And a pianist,
his hands in the air, plays a familiar keyboard.
He learned long ago by heart this music made now
by the vision of orange gems, sun staffs of violet,
rectangles of turquoise. A diva in a quavering voice
attempts to reach the highest note she sees
in the most vivid red, a brilliant shard as steady
as Macbeth's blade cutting through the scene.

On winter days the dim sun through this only
window lighting the parlor plays that pattern
of colors on the white wall opposite. "Variations
on a theme," one woman whispers, "in pianissimo."

When falling leaves from the tallow tree blow
across the window or the shadows of sailing birds
glide over the glass, they are seen as shades of implication
underlying melody and harmony, minor and major.

Likewise after a rain when clouds clear the sun, a few
transparent pieces of pure glass in the window live
with fire, flash in streaks like cymbals, like applause
igniting and spreading as the final notes fade.

Absent all these, it is understandable that only
the bravest, only the most foolhardy, only the resigned
should ever come to this window at night.

Now This Sound: *Ting Ting*

from *The Timekeeper's Dictionary of Musicology*

the slint of aborted rain
ceasing on the flagstone step
the dark
of light at the water spider's toes
as it swings sunward
cracked corn,
split pea
no and yes—scent of wild
mustard
no and yes—cello pizzicato
in the pines
the dent in the day
when the hair of the pawpaw blossom
pressures it once, twice
the stuttering
risk of April moving up the stem
of promise
Oriental princess and her ghost
in conversation
the stroke of the black
witch moth at 2 a.m.
life in the white eyes
of the white porcelain peacock
finger
cymbals removed and laid aside
a sequence
having nothing to do with before
or after
the first two names
of the first two stars

Art Gallery

Blue Series: Into the Deep Beautiful

1.

Hunters, believing in the salvation
of blue, dive into the deep, scuba
over reefs in search of blue coral,
or survey the coast for blue crabs,
ocean cliffs for blue-footed boobies,
open country for the blue-tongued
lizard and its language.

2.

Iridescent blue jellyfish in great
colonies drifted ashore last week.
The beach, covered with the tiny
blue sails of their dead bodies,
appeared as a surf of blue iris
in bloom, shasta blue butterflies
brooding on damp earth, wings
made of blue ocean poised
to rise again as saved souls.

3.

A wedding party carrying cakes
and flowers parades on the blue
cobblestone streets of Seville.
The groom yearns to discover the rare
blue pearls sewn to the ribboned
garter his bride wears for luck
beneath her silk skirts.

4.

"Although there are no actual blue
bats or blue bears, no blue poppies
or blue cockatoos, still it's possible
to gather blue flax, blue dayflowers,

to walk among blue spruce, blue-
jack oak, bluewood buckthorn, through
the verses of blue rains and thunder,"
so sing the garden statues at night
in their blue steel and marble voices.

5. Magic Carpet, the Third Coming

Without pilot, like the page of a book
tossed by the wind, it circles and turns
above the city roofs, the terraces
and watchtowers, around, upside down
and over the blue branches and webs
of winter, over plains of snow, blue as holy
white, beyond the razor blue of icy
fogs and faster over fields of bluestem,
banks of rita blues, spring azures,
the blue curls of camas and lupine
and on down, following the entire length
of that blue river flowing as if it had
parted the mountains to make this way.
We wave and watch through blue scopes
for a sign as it sails overhead, clear,
shining, and jeweled with the fading
summer light of a blue moon.

6.

A wise artist may spend her last
days seeking the silver of the blue
goose, the sizzling blue of the orange
sun sinking into the sea, the purple
grumble rising to the red howl
of the blue wolf, the deep delve
and gathering blue diamond of death.

Collage: Self-Portrait of the Artist at Work on a Series of Self-Portraits

In this portrait you see me with charcoal
and paper crouching in the sweet gum tree
outside her window, discovering her in sleep
as she dreams me covered by star-pointed
leaf shadows outside her window working.

Here I am sketching her in chalk
as she arranges her hair. She notices me
in the mirror, sees her pose emerging
on my tablet and changes her attitude.
I turn the page and begin again.

I am upside down painting her
as she appears upside down. I swivel.
She rotates.

I create her on canvas as she is created
in the eyes of a coyote across the field.
Her eyes glare with the coyote's own wild
foreboding. My painting captures the three
of us as one, staring in the same way
the Father, Son, and Holy Spirit stare.

Now I am forming her outline in pink neon
so that we may see her silhouette for the first
time at midnight. I shape the glowing bones
of each of my fingers as they work.

I have depicted myself as the moon
traveling with her like an artist of stone
light in the night. I cause stars to blink
off and on in the body of her vision. Here I am,
looking down from above, a god portraying

her soul as one single petal barely distinguishable
in the acres of the garden where she lives.

She determines. I occasion and record.
I find her again, creating myself portraying her
as a playing card on the table. Face up,
face down, I work in two dimensions—
the hidden, the revealed. I place my bet
and title this one *The Queen of Hearts*.

Portrait During the Creation of Sleep

Like the elm's shadow
disappearing at noon
into the trunk, branch,
and full leaf of its presence,
so Lila disappears in sleep,
becoming the fully bountiful
body of her body.

I say sleep is a place, the very
being of place, tangible,
alive. It is the suffocation
of the void from which breath
rises, the progenitor of *sleep*.

Lila closes her eyes, lays
her head on her pillow, moves
willingly, easily, as if to a lover,
toward the being of sleep.
She knows the way.

Like the power of the god
of absence, sleep transfigures
its creator.

No strumming wind, no surf,
no chitter or hum, no angelic
chorus—sleep, without sound
of itself, is the engendering
space of sound.

I say sleep is not faith
but all the atoms of faith
not yet united.

Lila lays her head
on the pillow, closes
the god of her eyes, lifts
like a shadow and disappears
into the full and boundless
forest of the sleep she sleeps.

Moon Deer in Winter: The Vision of Their Making

They rise up suddenly and sail
out of the frozen marshlands
and bracts, into the high black thicket
of the cold night with the same
reflective trajectory, the same racked
and wingless beauty as the moon.

These deer possessed the moon
long before the flashing white
tarpaulin of the sea possessed it,
before the myriad avenues of the mountain
snow returned it, before the hearts
of the albino cedars consumed it.

The geography of their alabaster
bones is far older than the moon's rock
spines and cratered ribs. Their silence
is more ancient than the moon's deaf
cuneiform. It was the steady grace
of their bounding that gave to the moon
the pattern of its landscape even before
it was present to receive such designation.
The scattered sheaves of ice they leave
in the rush of their flight predestined
the maps and features of the moon's
perpetual winter. It was their sleep
that required the missing side of the moon.

They have preceded themselves
by millenia in this moment during
which I watch them as they die

and rise again like the moon in its cycles,
as they sail alone and on purpose above
the marsh and straight into the light
of the moonlight in their eyes.

Seeing the Three Magi

They are country boys, dusty,
barefoot, bumping up a dirt road, one
pulling the wooden wagon, one riding,
the third behind pushing. They pause,
rotate places, continue on.

They are three summer winds—across
the bow, pressing the sails, skimming
the wake—following a ship following
a chart of stars.

On the street, one has a guitar
on his back, one a pair of drumsticks
hanging from his belt, the third
a mouth harp in his pocket.
They are wiser than the city.

(Three four-horned and cloven-footed
demons of the netherworld—demon
of blindness, demon of nightmares,
demon of faltering—attempt to track them
by moving beneath them upside down
and in the opposite direction.)

They are brothers sleeping
in a bed together beside an open
window overlooking the sea, a single
blanket pulled to their chins. The star
they dream as an angel of fire finally
rises, dripping and spilling light,
out of the eastern waves.

See those three white herons
descending with the nightfall, one

right behind the other almost like stars
over the black sky of the lake. In the beauty
and angle of their journey, doesn't it
make you wonder?

These three perfect yellow pears
placed on a table outdoors in the shade
of a winged elm—how intently they watch,
as though seeking, how steadfastly they pass
through the shadows of this day
on their way together.

Blue Series: Into the Deep Beautiful (the Sequel)

I. Fertility

Everything—purple lupine and laurel,
bush warbler, stellar jay and great horned owl,
swallowtail, red fox, snow thunder through regiments
of cottonwood and willow, blue ice on far lake waters,
summer shadows punctured by sun, even the day,
even you and I—all of these come and go,
but the sky remains, constant and encompassing.

II. Woman Riding a Tiger

She sits astride and rides him easily
as if traveling this way were what she
was born to do. She floats with his motion,
she a ship, he the sea. His shoulders
and haunches are an easy surf.

She needs no reins, no stirrups. Occasionally
she grasps the fur of his neck with both
hands. Her fingers disappear deep into
his pelt, hold to his beat and his current.

He moves silently in the way of cats,
not seas, like the shadow of a sea moving
with light across the day. They travel
unnoticed through the boulevards and shops
of the cities, the steam and smoke of cooking
fires in the camps. Nothing is disturbed
by their presence. No blinds close hastily.
No child cries out. No one rises. Not even
the black monkeys or the guardian birds
in the courtyards are bothered.

Crossing the open clearings, she glances up
at the sky where she sees them both reflected
in blue like the sea. They are a blue without
verge like the sky, without the boundaries
of bone or shore, without delineation. The blue
of his fur is deeper than the sea. Nothing can
infringe upon them. Like time, their journey
is the sky in the way the sky is not.

She remembers suddenly again
the moment when he swallowed her whole,
not the memory of violence, not the memory

of surrender, not the memory of release,
but the memory of totality like the sky.

Now she lays her head down
on his head. She stretches on her belly
the full length of his threshold, becomes
his bearing. She sees with his eyes
as they enter the blue gates of the prophecy
through which their god is passing.

Symposium Center

Garden Colloquy

"What the Flowers Tell Me,"
Gustav Mahler's Third Symphony, Second Movement

I. The Bearers of Flowers

Gathering and gathering all morning,
walking among the rows of the flower farm,
he has two big baskets of them strapped now
side by side to his back and one balanced
on his head. All are filled above their rims,
blossoms of white narcissi, blue flags,
honeysuckles, sweet pea dangling, spilling
occasionally to the road around his feet.

Who can deny he is a vastly different man
today than he will be tomorrow when his baskets
are loaded with paving stones, red rocks
and chat taken from the riverbed?

      ✿ ✿ ✿

Terra-cotta pots shaped like goats
and geese, turtles and cupids, bear flowers
in the spaces where their bellies
should be. I once watched a mountain marmot
eat yellow petals from a stem, thus bearing
for a while a coneflower in his real belly.

      ✿ ✿ ✿

Some people bear flowers by symphony,
by violin, by tambourine or flute, performing
The Song of Moonflowers, A Serenade
for Gilliflowers, or The Festival Overture of Wild
Petunias and Phlox. How strangely their fingers
and breath sustain those blossoms.

* * *

One widow places double glory lilies
weekly in the shiny bell of her dead
husband's French horn propped up
in the parlor corner.

* * *

In the library of a horticulturist,
many shelves bear the books of the sweetbriar
rose and the cabbage rose, the encyclopedias
of the mock orange and the Indian sorrel,
five legends of the woodland strawberry, plus
leather-bound copies of the history of catmint,
an atlas showing the migratory routes
of night-flowering cacti through the desert,
the journeys of lespedeza from field to field.

* * *

I wonder which came before—those
possessing the potential for bearing?
or the flowers, in first being
that which can be borne? or the bearer
of all flower-bearers and flowers,
the archetype from whom all bearers
and borne flowers must take their definition
and form? or anyone engaged in the act
of bearing flowers, without which act
there could be no archetype at all?

II. The Meaning of Fare-Thee-Well

The most tender of beings, whether whole
in themselves and singular—iris, morning glory,
orchid—or multiple in clusters—hyacinth,
laurel, purple saxifrage—they are vulnerable
to the slightest footstep, destroyed by the merest
scatter of late spring, early autumn, frost. Even
in summer moonlight, the first night air is too
harsh for many of them to bear.

          ❀ ❀ ❀

Yet they are gathered up, given to ill
and broken bodies as if they possessed the power
to cure solely through the fact of themselves,
as if the mere sight of lilies or jonquils could be
a remedy, a deed of healing alive inside the cells
of each of their momentary pistils and stamens.

          ❀ ❀ ❀

Greenhouse blossoms, gold and violet mums, red
and coral gladiola, are carried deliberately out
into the swift gray sky of winter, through cemetery
gates, left on snow as offerings against the hardest
hurt. Maybe a revelation of relief actually resides there,
created by the vulnerability of petals against ice.

          ❀ ❀ ❀

So near to oblivion themselves, almost illusory,
they are laid, nevertheless, by the hundreds
against the roughest stone markers, placed against
impregnable steel monuments, found buried,
shriveled and sere on the bones of ancient ancestors.

Remember the legend of Joseph's staff,
how it suddenly flowered, fragrant and brilliant
with white and fuchsia lilies when he placed it
before the priests, this miracle of flowers
a signal of God's favor.

Imagine it. Why daisies, why bluebells given
as penance for error, why primroses, why tulips as hope
against the bleakest turn, why baskets of them
overflowing, spirea, honeysuckle, given as belief
that the most intractable of wills could be altered?

Leaf-line, perfume, petal slope, pollen
powder, honey and swill—they are
their belief. Touch it. Even Cain might
have fared better had he tried these first.

A Philosopher of Verbs and Their Godliness Contemplates First Causes

Be is immortal, having given rise
from its immortal state to granite
and gnat, to cod, burr, skink, motmot
and bushbuck. Similarly, *stalk*
is the enduring reality, leopard being
merely its passing result, coyote
its temporal manifestation.

Grip and *swing* existed at the beginning,
necessitating woolly monkey as vehicle,
opossum as example, designing
the trapeze artist and her soul.

I contend that neither hawk, turkey vulture
nor barn swallow, neither porpoise, flying
squirrel, rattling tissue-paper kite, nor seed-
flag of thistles nor spore of filmy ferns,
could ever have existed without *soar*
and *sail*. *Coil*, as well, gave birth to pea vine
and snake, *scavenge* to hyena jaw, jackal,
herring gull, half a hundred hungry crows,
ubiquitous rat.

What else but *roll* is the defining
form in a midnight thunderhead?
What else but *roll* alone engendered
the vision of the surf, was first
in the first hub of the first wheel,
predetermined the shape in the sound
of its own English name?

Stars come and go but *adhere*
and *bestow* remain forever.

Imagine how springbok and pronghorn,
with their lithe hooves, their grace
and spine, were fundamentally formed
around the eternal suggestion of *leap*.
Shouldn't we say that in no way could salmon
have been salmon before *leap*? Yet *leap*
without these and without bullfrog airborne
from reeds to mid-pond, without the circus
of late August grasshoppers, the nuance
of a *grand jeté*, remains without science or art.

I wonder how long *cavort* was present,
yet void, before otter gave to it reason and place.
It must have taken eons for *laugh* and *cajole*
to come from eternity into life.

In the end who can doubt? *Praise*
is the underlying precondition compelling
the fact of two hands raised, open, palms up.
I, as philosopher, now know and do declare:
my creator is *seek*, my wisdom is *love*.

Correspondences

Wasn't it true once that I spoke
with the nocturnal expressions
of the blind snake emerging on a craggy
mountain slope at night, its cylindrical
body a silver motion in the rain
among the rocks?

Didn't I describe the virtues
of the moon jellyfish with the same
rising and descending measures of its flaring
blue circle of silk beneath the sea?

What I said of the bristlecone pine—
split and garbled, a crone cracked dry,
bent and scarped—I said not to the tree
but by the crippled fractures of the tree.
And because they and they alone
implied it, I said of field grasses
in the wind: *the rolling light of their*
fading brown and wine winter hues.

Didn't I repeat the stalking air
of the forest in the cadence of the lynx
tracking through snow? And in recounting
the draw of the barren uplands, how
could I avoid the sway of the plover's
low, soft moans of courtship?

The black centerpoint of the cat's
eye widens with concentration
until it fills its space fully, just as
the attentive night widens the moment
to the edges of its full horizon.

If the *see-you* song of the yellow-
toned vireo is the lilt of the leafy
brush where it perches, if the green
current of the sandy pond bottom
is the song of the sunfish holding
above its nest, then can the notes
of nothing by itself ever be known?

Any prayer of the evening sky—swift,
transparent, traveling beyond blue—possesses
all the vacant and wordless features of that
to which such a prayer may be offered.

An Art of Interactive Art

I. Selections from the *Book of One Glyph* ⊙ *with a Hundred Definitions*

This glyphic circle with a dot in the center
represents the sun or, occasionally, a crow's
eye, sometimes jubilation left in the ring
after the circus has departed or, depending
on context, consciousness piercing bliss.

In certain stories it stands for the seed
of a winter storm germinating over the Arctic,
a roundtable discussion of silence, a bullet
and the wake it leaves behind it in the blue sky.

In the musical scores of religious chants,
it indicates both the moment before the gong
is struck and the moment immediately after.
When appearing alone, it always means drought.

On any page it might be translated as a newborn
musk ox surrounded by the herd or the tunnel
of night the bat seeks. Or it can be read
simultaneously as the first thought of the hunter,
the dream of the snow hare in hibernation,
the flaw buried in a syllogism. Reading
with such possibilities is always a creative act.

Complete within the multiplicities of itself,
this one glyph is its own cosmology—hope
as it exists on the surface of the moon, dove
in flight disappearing into the symmetry
of peace, self-portrait of the earth's orbit,
"a voice crying in the wilderness."

II. And This Single Glyph \ or One Way of Looking at Sixteen Metaphors

the path of rain down a window,
the line of a train's whistle against
a prairie sky, the descent of sorrow, green
cicada rising from a sycamore at dusk,

mouse tail hanging from a cat's mouth,
the orchestra conductor's gesture
urging pianissimo, the scent of April
ghosts in a garden buried in snow,

multiple in the blue-green brushstrokes
in Van Gogh's *Self-Portrait*, multiple
in the arms of the chandelier in Vermeer's
Allegory of Painting, the length

of silence upon entering a dark room
at midnight, early morning campfire
without wind, dry autumn grass
within wind, a swan's neck as it lifts

from preening, the golden thread
of light appearing beneath a locked door,
the golden dangle of a broken web
at dusk, the scar down my father's face

III. Art, Music, or Everlasting Story

⊙, ╲, and ╲

come together as ⊙

I remember ╲, ╲,

╲ and ⊙

All that remains is ⊙

and ╲

A Seeker of the Undiscovered Pauses
in Contemplation

It might speak like fire or speak
simultaneously in multiple tongues
layered like a blackbird's feathers.
It might moan like evening. It might
raise its skirts like a jellyfish, turn
inside out, become wildness
and serenity upside down. *Must stay
alert.* It might blink out of existence
with each breath (should it possess breath),

be like a colored cathedral window
to the coming dawn at one time, a bird
to a hunter's blind at another. It may
be green when congealed, purple when
the wind, the fragrance of orange
in the morning, smoke beneath the moon.
Expect everything. It could sink like
a wave of the sea into the sea and rise
in the same manner. It could spin

like a whirlpool spins to a falling seed,
or like a star system, single or cluster,
is stationary to its spinning galaxy.
Must be watchful. It might be as heavy
as harvest or as light as a candle at noon.
Or suppose it is only the reflection
of whatever it encounters, becoming black
expanding when meeting dusk, a swelling
river beside a spring river, dead if death,
a question if questioned, me . . . if me . . .

Sanctuary

By and By, By and By

When you take me by my collar
and drag me down the road,
my heels bumping in the dust, my hair

tangled with bristles and burrs,
when you haul my body by one arm

up the narrow path dwindling away,
finally disappearing, when you prop me
on the summit like a rock on a cairn
and sprinkle rainwater on my face

to revive me, when you pry my mouth open,

fill it with grapes from your satchel,
wipe the red juice and silver sugar

from my chin and even the wind
among the boulders becomes a healing
lullaby, when the canines come

anyway sniffing and nudging, snarling

and baring their teeth at one another
and the large beasts begin their screaming

in the canyons and the little beasts
keep hidden and the sacred beasts
stare at the fading gibbous moon
as the summer lightning strikes itself

over and over inside the groaning black,

and you jerk me to my feet again,
pull me stumbling and falling behind you,

scraped and scratched down the switchbacks
toward the flapping sea flittering and singing
like flocks of meadow birds at dawn,

then, should you hear me ask again,
at least look me straight in the eye.

The Persistent Reality of Reality

To possess a small room alone,
a private garden, cool, still, fertile,
a room with a white wooden desk
against one wall, sheets of paper
in a pile, pens like a bouquet of stems
in a green glass jar, and on a shelf

above, leather-bound books, brass
clowns as bookends, comedy/tragedy,
a metal tear on tragedy's cheek,
and a ceramic figurine—March Hare
looking this way, Mad Hatter
the opposite, Dormouse to the sky—

an oval mirror the size of my hand
propped on a wire stand; and in one
corner of the room a white rocking
chair, a linen-shaded lamp, basket
beside it, needles, thimble (mending
of ritual), silver snipping scissors;

a place where one might sit and work
into the night at a piece in progress,
carefully stitch by stitch with satin
threads to sew a scene—a purple rosette
of prayer, a chant of bee-filled lilac,
a copper toad singing in its shrine;

to enter such a room, shut the door
and be locked away, to linger alone
in particular silence sitting at the desk
sewing scenes or in the chair rocking
into existence behind closed eyes
a woman in a white chair in a room

rocking back and forth, a woman neither
knowing, nor caring for a single instant,
of the ripping speed and vast rending
collapse into furious light of the frigid
black surrounding, that violent reunion
and growing shatter of the mad

beyond through which this woman,
this room, and its purpose (having thus
been acknowledged and so uttered) must
certainly now race forever.

At the Still Heart's Core

to go down into the earth,
down into the calm, redolent
depth of den or burrow,
to be hidden away, breathing
the cool, ash-mineral fragrance
of sunless soil and stone,

perfect, the subterrane,
the underground chamber,
the stolid rock cave, no rough
rush of wind, no heavy mob
of flailing leaves and sticks clashing
in a thunderous blow, no strident
commotions of yipping and barking
or shrill screeches of drunken
courting, no frenetic scratchings
and diggings and flingings of dirt
or hoof-gouging panics, the firmament
free of crazed and buzzing swarms,
whirring flocks and flittings, stings
and pinches, devoid of dizzy seeds,
dusty spores, spurs, squealing sirens,

purest night, no dawn, no dusk, maybe
a cold white toad the size of a toenail,
maybe a blank, blind spider suspended
catatonic, maybe a hairy residue
of fox kit or a crumble of tiny skeleton—
lost newt desiccated, lone mouse
spiked and taken years ago—
maybe a charred rock, a scatter
of burnt wood in splinters,

to lie down in communion
with the inert, becoming intimate
with the profundity of the immobile
and the mute, side by side with that
which has no purpose, the dry cracks
of hard packed earth, the crevices
of unresponsive rock walls, to sleep,
curled around the only quest, the only
flame there: my own deep-rooted,
wildly blooming pleasure at being
among those possessing no flicker
of ambition of any sort

For the Moral of the Story

For crags, for any bold, black, sharp-edged
chaos of broken rock, for pilings and high
cracking boulders and scrabbles, supreme
rising ridges, violet and buff-brown cliffs
and buttes and bluffs and deep-to-the-river-
bottom old canyons, silent, unmoving miles
and miles of granite alps and sandstone spikes,
useless peaks and impassable, deaf, mute,
without blood or breath or tongues, needing
neither sun nor night, needing no food, no
shelter, no offering, taking nothing—for all
of these that will not survive but will maintain
their fate perfectly until the last-left gust
and spiral of windblown sand has departed.

The 7th Day, Where God Rests

Rest here in this quiet. Lie down
in the absence remaining after summer
abandons the bindweeds, the yellow
rattlebox and the hedge apple
of the grasslands. Sleep here,
in multiple where each fallen
leaf of ash or elm once hung
from the branch.

Lie down inside the vacancy
existing in the sky where before
the downed stave oak stood,
or in the empty tunnel through
which the full moon monthly rises
and falls and disappears.

Nothing will disturb inside the remnant
cup of the sanderling's hatched egg,
in the pea pod shelled, in the yucca
hull split, windswept clear
of seeds and left hollow. Repose
in these cradles unbothered.

Here also is peace—curled inside
the skull-bone of the buck deer's
skeleton. Within this realm
the entire heaven surrounding
is solitary white and near,
brain-creased, antler-marked.
Ease to bed, somnolent all night
and all day of this declared day.

And enter my body, deserted,
deprived at death too, I pray. Occupy

that poor space, still and silent
as autumn earth beneath wet leaves,
as fossil stone in sun. Sleep well.
Bring dreams of waking.

This Day, Tomorrow, and the Next

When someone blind and someone deaf
walk together into the forest, one of them
understands the blackness of light
on a clear day. The other understands
the deep reach of stillness in a riot of green.

Both alike feel on their faces
the floating threads and tatters
of occasional sun passing through
the canopy of overlapping branches,
close thatch of needles, uneven roof
of broad leaves. And both can name
the fragrances of sweet sap and damp
soil, sodden cones, rain-filled mosses.

But neither encounters the burrow
of the fungus beetle leaving her eggs
in the dank of a fallen fir. Neither
is aware of the yellow of the jewelweed
to come. Neither is aware of the taste
of the salmonberry to be. Neither imagines
the spirit-deer made of thicket shadows,
the deer known only when imagined.

Within their inevitable errors
each regrets, each beholds.
Both put their hands the same
into the snow waters of the creek,
the flow pushing equally against
the pressure of their place.
But only one tilts toward the single
twitch-sluff of ground leaf where
the red newt slides. And only

one of them finds and lifts the red
newt from its rust-red leaf.

Each can hold a river-smooth
rock, feel the circle-leading allure
of its edges, remember by finger
and palm the shape and heft
of before the beginning. Within
their frailties, each asserts, each fears.

And for a brief moment either
of them might conceive and come
to love that which exists solely
as the possibility of radiant
green fern-leaf fronds spreading
over the forest floor, yellow-green
and black-green fir and cedar,
hemlocks filled with hanging moss
shags, the possibility of a ruffled
spill of lichens, the rip of a steel
blue creek, the chip *zeet* of dipper,
the slow swing of morning fog
up the hillside, conceive and love
that possibility alone which attends
steadily without ears and watches
forever without eyes.

Sensual Deprivation

I've never held a monkey of any kind,
never smoothed the stubbled fur
of a collared titi's head or enclosed
the twig-thin bones of a spider monkey's
fingers in mine or followed the wrinkled
petal of its primrose ear by touch.

Though I've held a live chicken hen
full grown, I've never put my finger
under the feathers of an eagle's breast,
felt the kind of furious flutter
that must thrum there continuously
as it sails in surges above the buttresses
of sea cliffs or down the thunder
of river ravines, that hot, pulsing
thunder under its skin raging
even as it roosts, even all night
under a dissolving and rainy moon.

I've never pressed the ball of my thumb
against a common wombat's claw
or felt the spotted cuscus curl its pink,
naked tail tip around my finger
or pressed my hand to the bass-drum
barrel of a sea lion's ribs as it bellows
or let the tentacle of a short-finned squid
suck to my fist.

What of essence can the eyes alone
truly perceive, those overrated, flighty
skimmers? After all, it was the hands
that invented fondling, the fingers
that created gentleness.

And I, who actually claim
to know you, have never once studied
with my finger the intricate assertion
of your inner wrist, have never found
your stance from neck to feet, every linked
furrow and tone, by touching them all,
or felt your breath as proof on my fingers
during a shrill snow closing in
on a day like this one.

What can I know, possessing now a touch
so restricted, a grasp so limited?
Such ignorant hands, such poor,
deprived fingers, such a pitiful,
hampered heart.

Love Object

I would give my most thoroughly steady
devotion to the gold glory of the moon,
except that the moon is insane
with fading, with falling away
and disappearing, gone, here,
and gone again, in its reception
of promises.

I would give all of my rapture, all
of it, to the chanting motion of the wind
inside kneeling grasses, inside swaying
snows, except that the wind has no
tongue of precision with which to praise
or cherish such ecstasy.

My body—up my legs, beyond my waist—
I would give without restraint to the fine
fingerings and searching caresses
of the river, except that the river's hands
are rippling light, vanishing flickers,
never the same hands, always new
strangers twiddling around my hips,
along my breasts.

I have expended levels of passion
on canyon cliffs and the careful sculpt
of their sky-thrusting walls, but they always
stare themselves, anyway, so perfectly
and continually right into stone.

Breathe my name in my ear, my own,
my own name back to me, like me.
Close my hand in yours, the same,
as only you.

Being Loved by the Insane in Love

They adore tiny features—the way
a lovely lash curves at the edge
of the eye like a single thread of upland
grass curves at the margin of the distant
sky, or the dependable habitation of the knuckle
of the smallest toe, intense as a fact
of history in its stance and diligence.

They often forbear any cruelty
to be allowed to listen to the lover
singing, "I go to the garden at night . . ."
or humming some made melody
never to be repeated. They themselves
when asked will sing the bell tones
of tree frogs or the single surf
sound of barnacles at high tide.

They will, for the pleasure of the lover,
imitate the calls of snow in wind,
June rising over its boundaries, the flutter
of airborne paper kites, the continuous,
faint tenor of sunlight touching
the outer planets of this place.

These are the languages of the insane,
the means and manner of their sex.
The increasing complexity of their love
is like space overlapping moments
inside rings of rain on a still surface
of lake, suggesting simultaneous
being and abyss.

They name every star they see
after the one they love, each so apt,

being mythically distant, being so deep
in spiral and plane, and they solicit
god to save the same.

They bring gifts of freedom,
like the shadows of birds at dawn,
luminous, transparent across the white,
curtained window, like the shadows
of swallows seen underwater
on the rocky beds of the streams
they follow, like the shadows of autumn
warblers moving in grief or desire
over the face of the one they love.

Leaving and returning without
warning or reason, like shadows too,
they make of their bodies gates
without latches or locks. For these,
their ways, in my certain sanity,
I seek to enter and pass among
the loving insane.

Whether or Not

We live in the mane of this great cat
and always have. We know how
to pitch our tight roots and tendrils
down into the warm mat of his long
and fertile fur and establish ourselves.
We latch on. We cling and nestle
and assume his rash and soothing scents,
the vast ameliorations of his domain.

Many of us are buried so deeply
and wonderfully in his superlative pelt
that we hardly remember his agile paws
and their pace, or the machinations
of his belly, or the gleam and spike
of his overwhelming warrior fangs.
We even believe our presence,
our various compositions and edifices,
our festivals and attentions add
a certain uniqueness to his bearing.

But we must take cover when this great
cat roars and glowers, when his saber-
claws appear with sheening and dash.
We quake and pray during that tumult.
We burrow deeper and tighten our grip
and wait it out whenever he shakes
his massive head, whenever he races
and leaps and all of our kind are tossed
and pummeled to and fro in the resulting
din. His fury rises always for reasons
that remain mysteries to us.

Yet we aspire throughout to the divinity
in his fierce, unapproachable eyes.

And when he rests his head, closes
his eyes and sleeps, we know peace
in the rock and low and mete
of his breathing, his occasional sigh,
the slight stretch, a quiver. And we wait
for each dawn of his waking when
he opens his eyes and sees again
and we are roused to that vision.

He hardly minds us in his grand
indifference. And we, in turn, ignore
his heedlessness. We ride with him willingly
wherever he goes and assume his glory;
for he is our great cat, our only cat, and we are his,
and he takes us where we could never,
in any shape or guise, go alone without him.

Theater

Three Conspiracies on Three Stages

I. The Stead

They soon came to the place,
often singly, occasionally an army—
wood-seeking beetles, spider
beetles, bessbugs, mud daubers
in the eaves, carpenter bees
and winged ants in the walls.

Some that came were sublime—
ivies and blooming vines, trumpet
and honeysuckle covering the windows,
morning glories curling the doorpost,
pale purple blossoms of kudzu
over the roof.

Some, like the milk thistles
and stinging nettles, chickweed,
pokeberry, blackberry, were rustic
and random in their approaches,
rooting in the abandoned grounds,
settling in the partial ruins.

Rags, rubbish, and wallpaper scraps
were torn apart, gnawed to pieces,
eaten by roaches, carried off by mice
and crows, for nests, for bedding.

After slow rains, the softened
and sodden structure and its easy
sinking into earth were attractive
to mosses, elf cap and silver,
molds, mildews, toadstools, snails;
the lingering moisture being also

conducive to rust on nails, hinges,
old keys hanging from tilting hooks,
a bucket, a washtub, the dog's pan.

All of these, and periodic storms,
of course, rocking winds, pellets
of hail, sleet, freezing cracks,
summer blisters, and pilferers too,
junk collectors, encroachers shooting
out windows, busting liquor bottles
for target practice, all of these,
the many and sundry, were as one
alone devoted to the end.

II. Turn of the Century

As recounted by a Swiss professor
of mechanics, it consisted of many
coordinations and detailed parts,
each carefully designed, crafted,
polished, lubricated lightly with oil
from the jaw and head of blackfish.
The shining cylinder, spiral spring,
the comb and its teeth, the bearings,
pins and driving spurs, all came
together in agreement, in harmony.

And when the key was wound,
the cogs catching, gears engaging,
the wheels and cylinder beginning
to turn, then, into an emptiness
not previously realized, music,
a living serenade, was present
at once among us like an unexpected
personage arriving suddenly
bringing astonishing news foreign
and familiar into the ordinary light
and shadows of an ordinary room
on an exceptional, late afternoon.

III. The Perspective of a Synopsis

The conspiracy was carried out
in the fine fashions of the time.
The leader of the assassins
wore a knee-length outercoat
of embroidered willow-green
damask, an inner coat of orange
satin, purple silk balloon trousers.

The two accomplices were cloaked
in black, ankle-length robes of velvet
lined with indigo feathers and fastened
across their shoulders by gold clasps
bearing the symbols of their order.
The glint of daggers hidden in the folds
of their robes could be seen now
and then as they crept across the stage.

The victim, taken by surprise,
murdered in his bed, was attired
in traditional nightwear of the season.

When the arresting authorities
arrived at the gate to perform
their function, they wore matching
scarlet felt hats and carried clinking
chains of polished steel. Locks
and keys dangled from their belts.
The high sheriff rang the bell
three times, paused and rang again
three times, as previously agreed.

The perpetrators were betrayed,
handed over—according to plan—bound

and carted off the stage in the final act
to the satisfaction and generous applause
of the audience dressed, one and all,
in the white of linen and lace.

The Hypnotist Speaks to His Origami Boat

You will remember afterward
    that you were simple at first,
        two-dimensional, static, unremarkable.

But see how I am folding you now,
    carefully, slowly, this way, that, peering
        and pressing. Feel how I fashion

your coming, smoothing the sleek
    curve of your sides. I am turning you
        upside down and back again, creating

depth for you, its rare hollow and yearning.
    I am taking you now, my darling, to the sea,
        holding you, the billow of your spreading,

in both of my hands, bringing you
    where you belong. You will balance
        perfectly here in this easy current,

riding slowly back and forth, the lull
    and the wane, as I recite to you in a whisper,
        rocking side to side, neither too far nor too

slight, as if the forces compelling
    this motion were both rude and serene.
        You are rising on each swell and surge—

one your desire, the other my answer—tipping
    almost but never forsaken. You are lifting easily
        and returning again and again. Our trance

in its steady state is a single moment
always passing. You are of the wind
and the perfume of the sea. You are chasmal

and buoyant, as consonant and willing,
as continuous as the drift of midnight
across the earth. I am slipping this candle

and its light into the heart of your belly.
You will remember this abounding. I am
watching as you disappear into the sky.

Now Playing *Truth and Fact*

The troupe of actors in the attic can be
a noisy bunch. They have a one-string
fiddle and a harmonica, and sometimes
during the full moon they gather around
the square of its light shining white
through their one window onto the floor.
There they sit singing of old times, often
mournfully like a circle of hounds howling.
They croon of when they were wise and dapper
gentlemen, lords and ladies, until one begins
to snuffle and one begins to snore and another
starts cracking peanuts and another sighs and fans
herself rapidly, and they all grow weary with
the nostalgia and decide to change the play.

During parade practice, the marching
and stomping round and round the attic
goes on for hours, horns, whistles, snazzy
cymbals. And what a commotion during war
rehearsals—the clashing of swords and shields
in mock battle, the roaring and fearsome
calls of the charge. The repeating fall
of bodies in fake death is worse than thunder.
The entire house trembles. The glass baubles
on the chandelier clink and rattle, and bits
of ceiling plaster float down like many
delicate moths settling slowly on the carpet.

The rehearsal of their scripts is continuous
all day—ravings of the mad king, wailings
of the lost lover, speeches before the guillotine.
Scraps and pieces of dialogue can be heard
beyond the walls of their mock drama. *Who goes?*

Throw the weasel out! Don't leave me
to die alone. Shut your trap!

The actors in the attic are a diversion
to families and lovers and even the lost,
all walking back and forth to town or riding
in conveyances along the boulevard.
Crowds gather to watch their silhouettes
in the high window, the posturing
and gesticulating, the fisticuffs, a flamenco
dancer, a gladiator, a two-person horse
pulling a wagon. The faces of players
painted green with garish red-rouged lips,
blackened eyebrows drawn in grimaces,
can be glimpsed now and then peering
out the window. Sometimes their faces
are obscured by the drooping feathers
of a broad-brimmed hat or hidden altogether
by a monk's hood, once by the slit-eyed mask
of a fanged panther, once by the beaked mask
of Il Medico Della Peste, once by a white
mask with no eyes and no mouth.

As evening darkens and the moonless night
lengthens, the crowd scatters, disappears,
and these dedicated actors begin to tire, discard
their costumes and their play, settle on their straw-
filled ticks, where one by one they leave the attic
to enter the stages where they are free to become
the black-angel and silver-goblin reflections
of the night, swift, soaring doves of fog traveling
over frozen rivers, ghosts of white wolves
changing to huddled rabbits changing to dunes
of shifting snow, sacred mistletoe hanging
from solitary trees, the tears of the moon,

the ice of Jupiter, free to become the true roles portrayed in the genuine dramas of their actual sleep, they themselves the perfect and only audience attending every performance.

In the Theater of Tomorrow, a Holy Spirit Contemplates Incarnation

"a hero or an insect . . ."

Dostoyevsky

I could be a merciful leader of men
or a glide of orange wings around sunny
openings in the daytime night of mountain
forests. I could be a blind poet reciting his work
or a blind white cricket calling in a cave.

I might be fair, wise, a judge
like Solomon, an essential justice among
gold and marble and the cedars of Lebanon,
or I could be a four-winged green lacewing
with copper eyes, hanging my eggs by silk
stalks to the undersides of meadow weeds.

I could build shelters for the poor.
I could be the blessing of a soaring
grasshopper dispensing airborne riot
to a dull afternoon. I could fix the starlights
of myself in the sky like Scorpio.

If I am Holy Spirit, then whatever carries
my spirit must be holy: a beggar
with a wooden bowl on the crowded
steps of a temple or squatting beside
a shrine along a pilgrim's way or a single
mayfly in a swarm of mayflies suspended
like a *yes* of silver in the sun for a day.

Whether a violet damselfly or a diviner,
I could lead the thirsty to clear springs.
Deep in the easy current at the bottom
of the pool, water mosses might be seen

blowing like a woman's hair freed
from its pins and ribbons. I could be
an underwater beetle in a crystal case
of air among those mosses. I could watch,
from below, the mouths of coon, lynx,
white-footed mouse, gray fox with kits,
as they dip their heads and drink.

A firefly carrying its pulsing torch
or a saint at prayer cradling a candle,
both highlight the disappearing expanse
of the invisible night.

I could sing the *Messiah* with a choir
in the loft of a cathedral and move the minds
of the people or be a katydid in a cage
of sticks delivering messages of certainty
to the sleeping or a high treetop cicada
transforming the silent leaves to a buzzing
chorus of green, transforming the sound
of summer to my own inherent *godspeed*.

Creation Alive

The trick is the trick the wild creature,
captured and caged, remembers and turns to,
staring as he does unmoving, facing,
without seeing, the bars of his cell and us.

He departs this place, enters the circling
archives and depths of his own body,
finds the woven forest, the damp rank
of its layered mat, the shadowed hues
and run of the river, cadence of its current
and cold, subtle peppery scent of cutbanks,
silty richness, soaked mosses, snailey
muds, the forgiving lap and sand of its bar.

He feels the imperceptible rise and fall
of the woods as a breathing he breathes
in sleep, haphazard slip of a leaf, jitter
of a twig, single hairs of hedge rubbish
and withered petals shaken loose by the wind
filling and bolstering all crevices and hollows
with the theology of its coming and going.

He pads slowly beside the moving waters,
sniffs the array of oak, hickory, sour mint,
markings and decay, hears a contrapuntal
play of fading caws in the distance, a closer
creak and rub of branch against branch.

He takes the fancy grasses of the clearing
into his mouth, licks the liquid sugar
of their graces. He is the light of the sun,
its pelt and paw, its crude warmth and rigor.

He creates its story in his passing. He makes
the sound of its soul. This is his name.

Step away and leave him. I know
you understand the trick. Study my eyes.

Natural History Exposition

Genesis: Primeval Rivers and Forests

If these weren't so very ancient,
they might easily be found. But they are
deeper than subterranean Siberia,
of a longer past than the oldest lichen
fossil discovered in Rhynie soil, from
farther away than found meteorite
remnants of three billion years.

These primeval forests and rivers
were the first to believe in trees dead
but standing. They were the first
to envision the living in the decay
of the down-dead, the first to conceive
possible orange rills of fungi, fluted
white helvella, beetles, spider mites
and spotted newts, a warty jumping slug
hidden beneath fallen needles and duff.

Birds were among them then before
there was flight, being mere wings of sun
off the rivers before there were waters, being
mere flitting shadows in the upper canopy
before there were leafy shadows or canopies
of flitting spirits or suns or ghosts of suns.

And although these ancient waters
flowing through storied rain forests
have never been told, I imagine how
they imagined before they conceived
fish as smooth as silver glass, fat
and buoyant on river bottoms, how
they dreamed those fish swirling
in schools of crystal to the surface
without yet having bones, with no

eyes of gold or scarlet gills, before
flood or drought, current or cutbank.

Today the hiss of a single stem
of seeded grass alone in a slender
wind recalls the silence in far rivers
and forests preparing for themselves,
a stillness expectant of wind, expectant
of seed. A brief fragrance passing now
suggests their beginning from absence,
the fragrance of the origin of fragrance,
damp oakmoss, sun on decay, the scent
of nostalgia for a thing I imagined
I knew before I knew.

Address: The Archaeans, One Cell Creatures

Although most are totally naked
and too scant for even the slightest
color and although they have no voice
that I've ever heard for cry or song, they are,
nevertheless, more than mirage, more
than hallucination, more than falsehood.

They have confronted sulfuric
boiling black sea bottoms and stayed,
held on under ten tons of polar ice,
established themselves in dense salts
and acids, survived eating metal ions.
They are more committed than oblivion,
more prolific than stars.

Far too ancient for scripture, each
one bears in its one cell one text—
the first whit of alpha, the first
jot of bearing, beneath the riling
sun the first nourishing of self.

Too lavish for saints, too trifling
for baptism, they have existed
throughout never gaining girth enough
to hold a firm hope of salvation.
Too meager in heart for compassion,
too lean for tears, less in substance
than sacrifice, not one has ever
carried a cross anywhere.

And not one of their trillions
has ever been given a tombstone.
I've never noticed a lessening
of light in the ceasing of any one

of them. They are more mutable
than mere breathing and vanishing,
more mysterious than resurrection,
too minimal for death.

Observe This Rock

As if this great rock were struck
by a magic hammer, birds are released
like fiery sparks in flurries of flocking
sapphire neon, flaming green, a purple-
gray aura moving upward in plumes
like smoke. As if wings and leaves
were one, they rise out of this rock
with seaside grasses, with grape ferns,
parsley ferns and roseroot. With pin oak,
laurel and bay, they soar and fall, swirl
mid-air and settle over and over.

Born of the ultimate silence of stone,
the weightless, sightless seeds and spores
of puffballs and cotton grass appear too,
floating from this rock, and likewise their kin—
summer swarming in the glassy double wings
of marsh dragonflies, death living as the white
filamented fungi of the amanitas.

As though it had been tapped with a sacred
rod, rivers spill from this rock, plummet
downward in gorges of vanishing rain. Morning
winds rush from the same crevasse, sweep east
and west. Flying fish leap up as if conceived
in the stone depths of a longing for sky.

Bulls, bison, gazelles and forest hogs, mules,
mountain goats, reedbucks bound forth
from the solid will buried at the center
of this boulder. Fear and riot remember
in the thousand explosions of their hooves.

Out of the staring idol of this rock comes
the vision of nebulae and their stars flaring
like evolving thunderheads lit from within,
scattering as notes of dust on fire across
the compass of the sunless black.

What is the voice of rock creating fire? What
is the thought of stone giving birth? Lucky
the house built on this rock.

Lightning from Lightning, I Said

Slice an apple. The instant the blade
pierces the russet-red skin, the knife
is knocked from my hand by the whip
of light let loose. Pluck a blackberry
off the vine and a bolt shoots out
like a needle of neon.

Rays explode outward in all directions
with each step the cougar takes crossing
the rocky hills. (I hear the distant
warning of thunder following.) The scree
of the white-winged hawk is a streak
of fire cutting through the heavens,
splitting them brilliantly, blindingly.
Likewise, fragments of shell left
at the nest reveal the jagged marks
of lightning at work in the hatching.

Similar to the sky, the desert at night
is lit with small fires too. Sizzling
spears of light burst forth as each new
bristle of cactus pushes from its sheath.
And many of us have seen the series of blue
electric bolts cracking hard, a cavalcade
of shocks, as a glacier breaks, calves,
crashes into the surging bay.

Cataclysms and upheavals are approaching
from everywhere. Think of lightning
in the thought of lightning. Even by
nodding our heads now, the "amen"
almost spoken, a blazing potential
is gathering, building, poised to strike.

There is an untapped power of light
lying dormant in each crystal grasp
in every splinter of snow falling tonight
over the icy valleys of the Himalayas.

Epoch Eocene: Another Stitch

Through the canopy of an ancient
rain forest in the China landmass of Asia
(wherever drifting Asia was on earth
40 million years ago), moonlight (the moon
a nearer moon than now) is broken
into jagged fragments by the overlapping
patterns of broadleaf and evergreen
shadow-shapes on the forest floor.

Not anyone from any sun or star system
would have seen her there, and nothing
living on earth then having seen her (perhaps
a primeval owl, a raptor hunting prey)
could have written:

The thumb-size primate is a quiver
trembling a leaf tip here and there
as she scrambles through the upper
canopy of the forest, her footsteps
as tiny and silent as the stars. Her infant
clings to the nub of her belly, nurses
at the speck of her nipple. She cradles it
as Mary will the Christ child. Her milk
is a better white than moonlight.

She licks the rich pudding of the insect
she catches and holds like a talisman,
her fingers the size of grains of rice,
her tongue as subtle and exact as a first
pinna of fern. She stops and stares
straight ahead, her eyes two moonpearls
in the closing black curtain upon curtain
of the forest, two moonseeds, the eyes
of her infant. She hisses, a thin hush,

shows her teeth to the night as branches
overhead rustle, scrape, and still.

A distant thundercloud revolves,
grumbling and sinking again and again
into its own deep descending riptides
and waves of gray. She disappears,
as the earth, lost in the arm of the galaxy,
turns steadily into the coming storm
(wherever the galaxy was then, wherever
the way, wherever the word).

Intimacy: A Lighting

Nothing escapes their touch. They fly
through the lifting fog above turbulent oceans and rising
freshwater marshes, wing through spring winds over fiery
sagebrush prairies.

They leave their pinprints in the sands
of Asian seashores, in the mud of backwoods river banks.
They take shelter in the skeletons of desert cacti, hold
in their bodies the patterns of the stars. They are Arctic
divers.

They perch on the barbed wire of ranchlands
and the spikes of prison walls, on clay chimneys
and the swaying masts of sailing ships. They survey
like sentinels from the tops of water towers and neon
signs, from the rules of solitary pines and crumbling
Roman lighthouses.

They follow shrimpers
and barges of garbage, pursue harvest reapers in flocks,
rest and feed among the scarecrow stalks and the refuse
of fallow fields. They alight on ice and sleep drifting
northward with the great bergs.

Leaving, returning,
they nest on the generous lap of Buddha's belly, inside
the folded hands of cemetery angels, in the belfries and eaves
of temples and palatial estates, roost under bleachers
and in the rotting rafters of abandoned barns and broken
monasteries.

They render. They imply. Their white
feathers against winter, their scarlet bodies against snow.
They touch everything.

And they ride, lifting ticks
and botflies from the backs of cattle, trail in the dust
of the herd, catching the scratch of locusts and beetles.
They scoop midges and gnats from the evening sky, fish
and squid from the bay, spear dewberries and elderberries
in brambles and thickets, snip seeds from grain grasses
and sunflowers. They dip their tongues deep into
the red of trumpet creepers, stir petals, lick nectar
and pollen and the honey myrtle. They open
their beaks to the rain.

At this moment somewhere,
they cling to a hunter's wrist, answer to a whistle, take
grapes from an open hand, perch on a bedpost, call
from a cage.

Their clucks and sweet warbles, whistles,
buzzes, and rolling chortles reminiscent of melting snow
rolling down hillsides, their chuckles, croaks, quacks,
peeps, pips and tinkling trills—they are everywhere an aural
scenery. They declare themselves. They denote. They rise
calling into the smoky skies over burning forests, into
the crumbling skies over war. Silent in sacrifice,
they come even into the gods.

They touch everything, covering
the circumference up and down, disappearing into the unmapped
interiors of hedgerows, into the recessed beams beneath bridges,
settling in cliff caves and niches behind plummeting jungle
waters, on the sheer rock walls above the drumming rapids
of narrow ravines.

Nothing escapes their touch. Like luck,
their shadows fall equally on the holy and the lost. The same
over sleep or rage, their silhouettes slide across the moon.

Boar: Even Though

He stumps along on his cloven hooves,
his midget legs, bulging, fat, 300-pound
pig, gorgeous, huge porker, jiggling
hams and haunches. He's surfeit,
an abundance of lean muscle and pure
lard, old feast in himself, a perfectly
fulfilled purpose in the flesh.

He stands for all of his swine relatives
and ancient ancestors of 10,000
years—warthog, bush pig, white-lipped
peccary, woolly boar, javelina, bristled
tuskers, acorn shovelers, river
swimmers, acute detectors of thunder
and lightning two days away, keen
routers of hidden truffles and tubers.

He adores his pignut hickories. He adores
his sows and their wallows.
He can sprint as fast as a squirrel.

Rolling and rooting, settling
into sleep, his great breathing body
inside his grass nest is such a mound
of steady heaving someone might believe
a hillock of forest were quaking to life.

His rumbling, guttural, reverberating
bass snorting, rising from the subterranean
depths of his barrel chest, is the kettle
drumroll of the generous earth
announcing its bounty: *Here he is.*
He eats anything—fungi, grasshoppers,

grains and garbage, eggs, snakes,
mollusks, birds, bark, manure.

Forgive his stink, forgive his beady,
squinty eyes, his ears like stiff hairy
handkerchiefs hanging over his brow,
his jutting teeth, his dripping digging
snout; for he possesses an intriguing
skull, a brain much superior to a cow's
or a dog's. And he is senior sire
of countless progeny, his seed so
multiplied "as the stars of the heaven."
He is provision. He nourishes.

Waddle-trotting away now, see
how his tail in its coil is laughing
at everything he turns his back on.

Whence and the Keeper

The Milky Way was created
by a herd of white horses
set loose, rearing and kicking,
galloping through the desert night,
leaving their white hoofprints
by the thousands upon thousands
across the empty black sands.

The Milky Way is a river of rising
rapids and frothy currents cresting
around bends, surging over white
boulders. It is a bridge of shining
ice cracking to pieces, slivers, chips,
gems, above a bottomless gorge.

That glowing arc, that band
of light is as ceremonious
as a congregation of luminous
plankton in a swirl of ocean current.
It is as devoted as a prayer
of pilgrims with lighted lanterns
moving across a barren valley
and up a steep mountain
to a future shrine.

Everything I see of the heavens,
I know by the earth. The Milky
Way is a pinwheel with four
spiraling arms composed of young
blue stars, old red stars at its bulging
center, and older citizen stars
of the ancient halo surrounding.

It protests war like a highway
of crushed and shattered bones,
promises like an avenue of white
violets and Easter lilies placed
for a funeral cortege, floats
like a wheel of white spiders
and ghosts of dandelion wings
scattered by a gust of cosmic
wind, sinks casually like coins
and strings of pearls tossed
from a carnival barge into the night.
By the earth I see whatever I see.

A Blind Astronomer in the Age of Stars

He considers himself lucky to have been born
during the Age of Stars, all those beings
in their shimmering shades, their silent,
untouchable presence. He imagines how
they shine as if they were the work of light
giving sight, like eyes, to a blind universe.

Making his way through fields at night,
he can feel the light from those million
sources touching him like the particles
composing the finest airy fog, touching him
like the knowledge of lives in a silent forest.
He feels each star in the way he hears
each syllable of his lover's whisper.

And he claims to see the constellations
from the inside out, having been inscribed
from birth, he says, with their configurations.
Indeed his Braille depictions of Canis Major,
Dorado, Lyra, Orion, are to scale and perfect.
Often through summer nights, he lies on open
hillsides to observe the heavens. He describes
the stars as transforming his body with their patterns
like tattoos of light—the wings of Cygnus,
the horns of Taurus. What kind of fortune
would it be, he wonders, to feel the light
of the Southern Cross along his brow?

He believes that the constant *jeetz-a-jeetz*
of the wayside crickets and the notes of the reed
toads sounding like whistles underwater
and the soft-bristle brush of grasses in the wind,
all together match in cadence the multiple
spacings and motions of the stars. He imagines

that the sudden piercing cry of a rabbit or a prairie
mouse at night corresponds to the streak of a falling
meteor, a helpless descending diagonal of light.
He hears their passing in this way. The earth,
he is certain, is related to the starry sky by blood.

By the solid black existing behind his eyes,
he understands the dimension beyond the edge
of the farthest horizon, that place whose light
has not had time to reach and touch him. He knows
that place, its state and its lack. One he calls
Patience, the other *Pity.*

Citizens in the Dominion of Heaven

They glide easily in and out among
the stars, the dying red giants
and wandering white dwarfs,
across rings of comets and moons,
past the flaring clouds and dusts
of stormy nebulae.

They sail in multiple patterns
at once, circular, orbital, spinning
and gyring. Even while sleeping,
daytime, nighttime, they fly,
their wings wide, weightless, invisible.
Their journeys are as common,
as deep and far as sleep itself.

They float together with flocks
of pipits and larks and locusts,
with stands of aspen, bee plant,
and little bluestem, with fallen stands
of fir and cedar and the heavy stalks
of winter marshes, with stands
of sandstone ridges and granite
bluffs, stands of wolves on the hunt.
They travel with the sun.

Inside pavilions, tents, caves
or parlors, attics or cellars, under
canopies, gazebos, porticoes
or latticed roofs, domed roofs,
or without cover of any kind, hatless,
coatless in the open sky, they soar
down hollows and bottomless
canyons, descending chasms

of absence. A smatter of stellar
fire burns in the distance beyond.

Even while a bell announces
morning, even while the hurdy-gurdy
man is playing and the balloon man
is hawking and the trapeze artist
swings upside down, even while
a window is closed against rain
and the table is laid, while winds
blow unwitnessed over the white fur
of arctic foxes, the bloody feathers
of silver geese, they all sail together
through the dim lights of novas
and quasars, through solar winds
of double suns and star systems,
through black energy and dark matter.

Their continual passages are as necessary
to life as the scriptures of blood. Being
so inseparable from it, they often
forget: the entirety of the heavens
has always been theirs.

Recitals and Rituals

1.

While all the stars through the starry
night sky were radiant as always
with the explosions of their great
central nuclear fires, the men cut off
the witch's hair to assure the devil
could not hide there.

2.

During the outdoor concert
of mandolin, harmonium and boys'
choir taking place in the city park,
and during the fireworks afterward
showering light in colors above the city,
all during the applause and the people
dispersing, the highest ice-field
on Jupiter's largest frigid moon
was silent and absolute, pale
against a bolder black, unmarred,
pure, without monument.

3.

As his horse stumbled up the muddy
bank, the soldier's spiked helmet fell
from his head and rolled into the river.
At the same time many zones away
a student taking notes at a lecture
wrote: *a white dwarf is destined
to drift in space for millennia.*

4.

Starlight, leaving Sirius A
in Canis Major at the moment
she publicly renounced her faith,

reached her eyes eight years later.
In that instant, she remembered.
Was this an echo coming as light?
or light coming as memory? the past
and present finally united? the same
moment of the event or another?

5.

The horseshoe crab carries in the pit
of each of its cells a sheer script composed
in the beginning by its own created
devotion, created before its compound
eyes, bulbous brain, tubular heart, before
seeking and decision, a devotion created
before creation, when naught was
the only sum. We can all remember that.

6.

If, at midnight on a summer solstice,
you look down into a rain-filled bowl
of any kind—flower or shell, hollow
stump or half-skull—down past surface
and descent, past reflection into sibilance
and on, down to the first star-thrash
of darkness, you will see how fathomlessly
perfect is god's conception of your home.

Acknowledgments

My thanks to the editors of the following magazines in which some of the poems in this book were first published.

Alaska Quarterly Review: "A Blind Astronomer in the Age of Stars"

Field: "Recitals and Rituals"; "Creation Alive"

Fine Madness: "Recitative from *The Ruby Plan,* Act I, Scene iv"; "And This Single Glyph \ or One Way of Looking at Sixteen Metaphors"; "A Seeker of the Undiscovered Pauses in Contemplation"; "Epoch Eocene: Another Stitch"; "Woman Riding a Tiger"

Flyway: "The Stead"; "Observe This Rock"

The Georgia Review: "Genesis: Primeval Rivers and Forests"

The Gettysburg Review: "A Philosopher of Verbs and Their Godliness Contemplates First Causes"; "Citizens in the Dominion of Heaven"; "Seeing the Three Magi"; "Intimacy: A Lighting"

Gulf Coast Review: "The Metal Lion and the Monk, a Percussion Quintet"

Image: "Boar: Even Though"; "Whence and the Keeper"

The Iron Horse Literary Review: "Portrait During the Creation of Sleep"; "Lost in the Heart of the Concert"

ISLE: "Moon Deer in Winter: A Vision of Their Making"

Janus Head: "Correspondences"

Margie: "By and By, By and By"

The Midwest Quarterly: "Now This Sound: *Ting, Ting*"; "The 7th Day, Where God Rests"

The Notre Dame Review: "The Bearers of Flowers"

OnEarth: "This Day, Tomorrow, and the Next"

Orion: "The Great Deluge and Its Coming"

Poetry: "Address: The Archaeans, One Cell Creatures"

Runes: "Whether or Not"; "Lightning from Lightning, I Said"

Washington Square: "Being Loved by the Insane in Love"

Weber Studies: "Sensual Deprivation"

Wilderness: "For the Moral of the Story"

My gratitude to the Lannan Foundation for a Literary Award that gave recognition to my work and support during the time when many of the poems in this book were being written. Thanks to Paul Slovak for his time, patience, and advice. I appreciate my days in the H. J. Andrews Experimental Forest and thank all those responsible for facilitating my visit there. My thanks to the staff, faculty, and students of the MFA Program in Writing at Pacific University, for their friendship and conversations.

John Rogers

Pattiann Rogers has published ten books of poetry, a book-length essay, *The Dream of the Marsh Wren*, and *A Covenant of Seasons*, poems and monotypes, in collaboration with the artist Joellyn Duesberry. Her most recent books are *Firekeeper, Selected Poems, Revised and Expanded* (Milkweed Editions, 2005) and *Generations* (Penguin, 2004). *Song of the World Becoming, Poems, New and Collected, 1981–2001* (Milkweed Editions) was a finalist for the Los Angeles Times Book Prize and an Editor's Choice in *Booklist. Firekeeper, Selected Poems* was a finalist for the Lenore Marshall Award and a Publishers Weekly Best Book of 1994. Rogers is the recipient of two NEA Grants, a Guggenheim Fellowship, and a 2005 Literary Award in Poetry from the Lannan Foundation. Her poems have won the Tietjens Prize, the Hokin Prize, and the Bock Prize from *Poetry*, the Roethke Prize from *Poetry Northwest*, two Strousse Awards from *Prairie Schooner*, and five Pushcart Prizes. In 2000, Rogers was a resident at the Rockefeller Foundation's Bellagio Study and Conference Center in Bellagio, Italy. Her papers are archived in the Sowell Family Collection of Literature, Community, and the Natural World at Texas Tech University. Rogers has been a visiting writer at numerous universities and colleges and was Associate Professor at the University of Arkansas from 1993 to 1997. She is currently on the faculty of Pacific University's MFA Program in Writing. She is the mother of two sons and has three grandsons. She lives with her husband, a retired geophysicist, in Colorado.

PENGUIN POETS